REMEMBERING:
THE DEATH OF A CHILD

SUPPORT *and* HEALING
HOPE *and* INSPIRATION

ROBERT R. THOMPSON, M.D.

SUGARLOAF
PUBLISHING HOUSE

Remembering: The Death of a Child

Library of Congress Control Number: 2002093130

Design by Lecy Design

Original Artwork on back cover
and on section title pages by Jill Neumann

Printed in the United States of America

First Edition

Published by
Sugarloaf Publishing House

For information:
www.Sugarloafpublishing.com

ISBN 0-9722942-0-1

SUGARLOAF PUBLISHING HOUSE

DEDICATION

To Paul's brothers, Andrew and Peter, and their wives, Wendy and Mayumi, who have suffered loss with us and helped us remember Paul and celebrate his life.

To our close family members, Mary, George, Aaron, and Elizabeth, who gave us their love and support.

To all the wonderful friends in our community and our church, who helped us through the most difficult and tragic event of our lives.

To the people of Compassionate Friends, whose organization, acceptance, and love gave us a forum in which to work through our grief and come to some peaceful accommodation to it.

And finally, to the memory of Grandma and Grandpa Lindquist, who loved us and cared for us, and who have since gone to be with Paul in the place we call Heaven.

ACKNOWLEDGMENTS

I would like to thank and acknowledge the following people who reviewed and made suggestions for this manuscript:

Andrew, Peter, and Wendy, for sharing their memories of Paul's life and death and reviewing the details for accuracy as well as making suggestions for certain portions of the book.

Mike and Alice Hickey, for coming to the house that first horrible day after Paul's death and introducing us to The Compassionate Friends and for their suggestions about the manuscript.

Shirley and Gary Hoyme who lost a daughter, Beth, and whose critique and suggestions were helpful to this writing.

Steven L. Channing of Winnipeg, Canada, for writing the foreword and contributing the poem which appears on page 96, making suggestions for the manuscript, and sharing the story of his daughter Kim's death.

John and Bobbie Maakestad, for their helpful suggestions and correction of the author's numerous syntactical indiscretions.

C.J. Delong whose own book, *Help is Here*, along with her guidance, helped steer the author through the publishing process.

Fellow sojourners, whose love and support sustains all who have lost a child.

And finally, Martha, for her willingness to tearfully revisit the details of Paul's life and death, and for her steadfast love and dedication to this project.

FOREWORD

Suffering the death of a child is the worst living nightmare a parent can be asked to face. Instantly, without a choice in the matter, the entire world changes—forever.

When my daughter, Kim, died my world was a confused mass of swirling colors and noises, none of which made any sense. Time became distorted and lost all meaning as I frantically searched for someone who could assure me it wasn't true. I even tried making a deal with God.

In the numbing days that followed, neither family nor friends could reach me. Outwardly, I hugged and cried, did the things that were expected of me, but inside, part of me died with Kim. Surviving the death of my child, my daughter, was not something I chose to do. It was forced upon me. I had to be strong for my surviving son, Dean. After the funeral, utter loneliness set in. I felt so completely lost and empty in my soul that I sat on my couch and cried out to my God, pleading for help.

Two months later, I was put in touch with The Compassionate Friends, Inc, of Canada. In their loving care, I found my way back, not only to the life I knew, but also to a broader, richer life. It was a life devoid of the meaningless entrapments that had once meant so much to me—life where people mattered more and time was precious.

In the first part of his book, Dr. Thompson relates the story of the tragic loss of his son. His experience as a father, husband, and physician allows us a unique insight. Often bereaved parents only have contact with the clinical side of their family doctor at the time of their loss. Dr. Thompson shares the personal tragedy of himself and his wife, Martha, in a frank and honest way that only a bereaved parent can understand.

The second part of the book offers not only hope but also clinical advice to the newly (and not-so-newly) bereaved along their path to emotional wellness. The choice to survive and recover is presented in a very compassionate way, leading us from the dark, through the fog, into sunlight. The advice on medication would have certainly benefited me in my early days of sorrow.

Finally, in the last part of the book, Dr. Thompson offers words which have touched his soul. I am honored that my poem, *Your Compassionate Friend*, was chosen to be among those words of inspiration. I offer them in memory of my daughter, Kim.

While none of us chooses to walk the path of sorrow and grief that the death of a child sets us upon, it is a part of life that can and does happen to anyone. The familiar adage "Time heals all wounds" is sadly incorrect. It's what we do with that time that determines if and how well we recover. Reading *Remembering: The Death of a Child* is time well invested in your recovery.

We can survive. It's what our children wish for us.

STEVEN L. CHANNING
WINNIPEG, CANADA

PREFACE

This is a story about the untimely and traumatic death of our son and brother, Paul Leslie Thompson (June 3, 1970 to April 9, 1989). It is a book about our shock and suffering and how we struggled through it with the love and support of family, friends, church, and the national organization known as The Compassionate Friends.

In telling our story we resisted the temptation to reveal more of Paul's personal life and his relationships in the hope that our story will speak in a universal way to those who have lost a child of any age or gender, at any time. We decided not to make this book a eulogy to our son but, instead, the story of our journey through shock and grief to, eventually, healing and peace.

In the sense in which the word *happy* is used by our culture, there can be no happy ending to such a story. There can be comfort and calm, however, and this book is about how we found ours. Our prayer for you is that you will find peace on your journey and some respite from your struggle.

ROBERT AND MARTHA THOMPSON
JUNE 20, 2002

"Whoever survives a test, whatever it may be, must tell the story. That is his duty."

ELIE WIESEL

PART ONE—THE DEATH OF A CHILD

PART TWO—SUPPORT AND HEALING

PART THREE—SOME PEACEFUL MEMORIES

PART ONE

THE DEATH OF
A CHILD

None of us can help the things life has done to us.

They're done before you realize it,

And once they're done

They make you do other things,

Until at last

Everything comes between you

And what you'd like to be,

And you have lost your true self forever.

EUGENE O'NEILL

CHAPTER ONE
THE CALL

Saturday, April 8, 1989, seemed like an ordinary day. As many rural family physicians do, I was making rounds at the small hospital in our town, having made arrangements to see some patients in the emergency room. I hoped to get a few problems out of the way and have most of the weekend to myself. At ten o'clock, as I was about to perform a minor surgical procedure on the wife of one of my colleagues, the charge nurse knocked lightly and peeked in the exam room.

"Your wife wants you on the phone," she said.

I'm sure there was some irritation in my voice at being interrupted. "Tell her I'll call her back," I replied.

"She said it was an emergency," she persisted.

Martha is not the kind of person who defines an emergency broadly. In my thirty-five years of practicing medicine she has called me only a few times during the day and almost always accepted a call back if I was busy. I knew something important must be up, but I had no idea of the shock I was about to get.

I excused myself from the room with apologies to my partner and his wife, took off my gloves and mask, and headed for the nurse's station. As I walked down the corridor to the waiting phone, several emergencies came to mind: our golden retriever, Daisy, might have been hit by a car; maybe there was a small house fire; or water in the basement. I don't recall even thinking of our three sons, who were all away from home. Andrew, the oldest, was living in Colorado working for the U.S. Fish and Wildlife Service. Later I would learn he was in the mountains on avalanche training as part of his volunteer work with the National Ski Patrol. Peter was a senior at Gustavus Adolphus College in St. Peter, Minnesota, and our youngest son, Paul, was a freshman at the University of Minnesota, Duluth. Paul had had some difficulty adjusting to college life, but now, in the second semester, was doing well. He was in Air Force

4

ROTC and had made a career decision to become a pilot. He had recently passed the written qualifying examination and was scheduled for his flight physical in two weeks. He had sounded so excited when he was home for Easter break.

I picked up the phone. "What's up?"

Martha's voice was amazingly controlled. "Paul's been in an accident...," she paused.

In that brief pause I saw broken bones, a ruptured spleen, a head injury, or, God forbid, a spinal cord injury. In my twenty-five years of medical practice I had seen death. I knew death. I knew it as a friend and welcome visitor, and I knew it as a hated and feared monster that crushed and dehumanized people. But now, in this brief moment of dread, I did not associate death with one of my own children.

After the pause, Martha said, "... and he's been killed!" Not that he was dead, but that he had been killed. I remember those words so well. Their violence tore through me like a high-speed missile. I couldn't respond. Nurses were looking at me, curious about what had prompted Martha's call. I'm sure the color drained from my face as I uttered an oft-used expression in my trade: "I'll be right there."

We didn't say it then or later, but somehow I think we both thought my physician presence would make things right. After all, isn't death but a combination of medical problems? And what is a doctor but someone to solve those problems? The mind-numbing denial was already at work.

I left the hospital without a word to anyone. I got into my car and headed home. As I sped down Mill Street, past the high school and the familiar row of homes, I saw nothing and thought nothing. It was as if my brain couldn't grasp the idea of one of our children dying. I turned onto the overpass and onto the gravel road to our house. I remember hitting the steering wheel with my fist and saying "No!" several times.

Somewhere during the five-minute drive from the hospital to home, I had a thought. It was to be the first and ultimately the most important realization in my grieving. I thought, "It's not about me. I'll live. I'll get through this. Paul won't. He didn't. His life is over. Nothing he ever dreamed of or hoped for will come to pass. We'll never see him again. He's gone forever."

Still no tears.

When I pulled into the driveway, the local police car was there, as if for a routine house check. I ran up the front steps and in the front door. The young officer and Martha were standing in the hallway. He looked pale and uncomfortable. It was no doubt a traumatic time for him—probably the first of many such notifications he would make during his career, if he survived this one. Martha looked blank and stunned as we ran to each other and embraced. Still no tears.

We asked the officer for details—When? Where? How?

"Auto accident near Duluth, sometime early this morning."

That's all. He didn't know any other details. He gave us the name of the sheriff's deputy in Duluth whom we could call. He managed to say that he was sorry to be the bearer of such bad news, backed to the door, and was gone.

We were alone, so alone, that dreary April Saturday morning. We collapsed in each other's arms and our bodies shook with the first waves of an ocean of tears. It was truly the first moment of the rest of our lives.

CHAPTER TWO
SHOCK

For most of that first day, it seemed as though everything took place in our kitchen. For one thing, that's where the telephone was. It was also the gathering place in our home.

I first called our good friend at his law office. Between sobs, I told him about Paul. He was at our house in five minutes and stayed, along with others, most of the day.

We felt so awash in tears and pain, and yet felt we had to find out more. Could it be a mistake? Where was Paul now? Who had our son? After a series of difficult phone calls, we reached the Douglas County sheriff's office in Superior, Wisconsin. His calm answers to our questions told us that he had been expecting our call. He told us that Paul had been a passenger in a car with two other college classmates. Around five o'clock in the morning, they were headed south out of Duluth on a county roadway. It was a clear day near sunrise and there was a patchwork of morning frost on the road surface. In an attempt to negotiate a curve, the car began to slide and fishtail. Eric, the driver, was able to slow the car and, after skidding about 400 feet, bring it nearly to a stop. Still moving slowly, the two-door Mercury Capri struck the top of a culvert and had enough momentum to overturn on its top in a stream. Although the twelve-foot-wide stream was swollen with spring snow runoff, it still had a one- to two-inch layer of ice covering it. The car sat precariously on the ice for a moment, perhaps as long as a minute, and then broke through, plunging into eight feet of icy water. Eric removed the keys from the ignition and put them in his pocket, as we were to learn later from Greg, who was the only survivor of the three boys. Paul was in the back seat and couldn't get out. He broke the rear window with a hockey stick but could not wiggle through the opening. Somehow, Greg climbed over Eric and swam out through the open driver-side window. The passenger-side door was closed when the car was retrieved, and the window was shut.

Greg swam to the surface, exhausted from his struggle, and collapsed on the bank of the small stream, waiting for Eric and Paul to follow. He remembers seeing the headlights of the car shining below the water's surface. He considered momentarily whether he should go back into the icy water and attempt to get his two friends out of the car. Ultimately, and correctly, we believe, he decided he couldn't do it. Instead, he climbed back to the road and attempted to get help. His appearance and staggering gait probably discouraged the infrequent cars from stopping. He was most likely already suffering from hypothermia. One by one they slowed down and then drove by as he tried to hail them. He doesn't remember how long he walked north along the county road.

Finally, someone stopped and asked if he needed help. He must have been a sight and confused as well. The unknown Good Samaritan drove him directly to the hospital and dropped him off. After he rewarmed and told his story, perhaps as long as an hour after the accident, the sheriff was able to locate the stream. Without Greg's directions, the sheriff later told us, he would not have been able to locate the site, and, once there, he would not have seen the car. It was invisible below the surface.

As Martha and I listened to the painful details of our son's death unfold, we were too stunned to ask many questions. I finally asked the sheriff the obvious question, "So then, Paul drowned?"

After a pause he simply answered, "Yes, he drowned."

Our acute pain and grief attacked us in waves. In between tears, we tried to comfort each other. We embraced and held on to each other tightly. Then the phone or doorbell would ring. Word was getting out quickly in our small community, and friends were coming to the house or calling. Our minister, whom we consider a good friend, and our lawyer friend were sitting in the living room. They supported us with their presence, but clearly, like us, didn't know what to say or do.

We were alternately immobilized by our suffering and consumed by wanting to know more specific details. Most importantly, we wanted to know where he was. It seemed as if in knowing the details of Paul's death, we could somehow undo them and bring him back to us. Of course, we didn't really want to believe what we were hearing and I think, in retrospect, this was a healthy struggle. The will to not give up or give in without a fight set the stage for our adjustment to our loss and was ultimately how we kept it all from overwhelming us.

The phone, the doorbell, the voices, and the crying presented a cacophony of grief. Through it all we had to call our sons and both sets of parents, as well as brothers and sisters and other relatives. Each call renewed the shock for us as we eventually had to speak the original bad news: "Paul's been killed."

Stunned silence, followed by, "What?! No!" or, "Oh my God. How?" How, it seems, made a difference to everyone.

Peter's college roommate was with him. How do you tell a son his brother's been killed? There isn't a good way, I can tell you that. With a friend driving, Peter began the ninety-mile drive to our home.

Andrew was another matter. We contacted the ski lodge where he had gone for avalanche exercises with the ski patrol. We were told that the group was in the mountains and perhaps could be reached by radio when they got within range. Thus it was much later that evening when we were finally able to talk to our oldest. He had to drive to his home in Grand Junction and then fly to Denver for a flight to Minnesota the next morning. We all wept as we told him the details on the phone, as we knew them. We longed to hold him and give him strength but we couldn't. We contacted a Lutheran pastor in Grand Junction who called on Andrew at home—a debt we were never able to repay—because we couldn't bear the thought of him being there alone. We at least had a supporting group of family and friends to help us, but Andrew had no one.

One other important event of that day stands out in my memory. Our local funeral director, a friend of ours, left town immediately upon hearing of Paul's death to transport his body home to a loving family and a warmth he would never again feel. Both Paul and Eric had autopsies performed as required for all traffic fatalities by Minnesota state law. After the autopsy, which later we would learn only revealed death by drowning, Paul's body was taken to a Duluth funeral home, which released it to our funeral director.

For Martha and me there was a feeling of unreality mixed with the pain of our loss. We had not, in our hearts, accepted Paul's death. We needed to see him, feel him, and hold him. Somewhere in the deepest recesses of our mind was the notion that his death was not final, and therefore reversible, until we saw him. Jim, our funeral director, and I had worked together on many deaths. I was deputy coroner for our county and had crossed paths with Jim over the years as we investigated fatalities of all types in our area. Car accidents, suicides, natural deaths, and a few homicides had brought us together. We had both become somewhat professionally inured to death in all its grisly forms. Families and loved ones struck down and struck dumb by shock and sorrow were not new to us, but this was very different for both of us. Jim hated to deal with untimely deaths of young people, and it was clearly hard on him to have to do it. Always his professional demeanor prevailed, but I'm sure that, over the years, such deaths and funerals took their toll on him. Jim called when he arrived in town with Paul's body.

"Jim, we have to see him," I said. Martha was already putting her coat on.

Jim paused, and I could tell he was reluctant. "He's not dressed, Doc," he said.

"Well, cover him with a sheet—we're on our way," I replied. And with that, we were out the door.

Minutes later we walked in the front door of the funeral chapel. Jim was alone and, after greeting us warmly, ushered us into the back room where Paul lay on a gurney covered with a sheet from the neck down. He looked for all the world like he was sleeping. His light brown hair, recently cut, was in place and his color, while not flush with the pink of youth, was not the ashen gray of death. Martha and I held each other as we walked slowly toward him. Jim left us and we were alone with our son, ten hours after his death.

If we had felt pain and shock before, now our hearts were ripped from their moorings. We literally held each other up as we stroked his hair and kissed his forehead. Martha's words are as vivid to me today as they were twelve years ago.

"Oh Bob! It's him! It's really him!"

Paul, as we knew him, had ceased to exist. Now we knew it for sure—it was written forever on our hearts.

His birth flashed before me. Martha and I had brought him into the world together in 1970. In a small rural hospital in western Minnesota, when it was still possible to do those things, it was just the two of us and a nurse in the delivery room. We had similarly delivered our second son, Peter, three years before in a small hospital in an Alaskan village on the Yukon River without any physician backup, so Paul's birth seemed like a piece of cake. When I saw it was a boy (we couldn't predetermine gender in those days), I exclaimed, "Our three sons." He weighed over nine pounds and had only a few wisps of hair that would later become so blonde it looked white. As Martha and I admired our squalling handiwork, we had no inkling of the tragedy that would befall him nearly twenty years hence.

I don't remember how long we stayed—maybe only ten or fifteen minutes. I know we were reluctant to leave Paul alone. But whatever journey he had embarked upon, whatever abyss exists between our fragile lives and death, we knew he had to go alone. We wanted to go with him, support him, shield him, and encourage him, but the limitations of our lives prevented it.

Jim walked us out to our car and we drove slowly home, knowing that our goodbyes would have to be said mentally and spiritually. We recalled together that when Paul had left for college after being home for Easter break, I had stopped by his room. We'd said goodbye, embraced, and said "I love you" to each other. Martha recalled that those were his last words to her also. We sought, and found, some small speck of comfort in those recollections, but not nearly enough.

We returned home to a house full of friends and family. Martha's parents, then in their early eighties, had made the six-hour drive from Illinois and were there to start the tears flowing again. We recalled more Paul memories and stories as we filled them in on the details of the tragic, freakish moment that had taken away one of their six grandchildren.

The rest of the first day was filled with the presence of friends and associates who came to the house with food and comforting words. They were supporting us by the only means they knew—by being there. Their words are not recalled, for it was not their words that mattered, then or now. Some could not speak at all. A close friend, whose daughter had been a classmate of Paul's, tried to speak several times and could not. After several tries he sat on the couch, mute and angry with himself that he could not console us. We consoled him. We consoled each other. Touch seemed so helpful. Handshakes were not enough. Embraces were required, and each hug squeezed out a new burst of anguish.

The cold darkness of early April gradually enveloped us, adding but another layer to our shroud of grief. Friends embraced one more time leaving behind their final thoughts and casserole dishes. Only family remained. We talked with Andrew, still on his way home, several times and tried to reassure and comfort him, but how could we? We could not even comfort ourselves, let alone Paul's brother, fifteen hundred miles away.

Peter, Grandma and Grandpa, and Martha's sister, Mary, sat around the table. The table around which we had shared so much was not for eating now. It provided a place to be, not to do. Indeed, what was there to do?

Martha and I both discovered we had severe headaches. We had not previously been headache sufferers but we had never cried so much in such a short time. The headache was frontal, behind the eyes, and best described as throbbing. It would recur with more severity each time there was a new episode of tears.

Finally, perhaps around midnight, Martha and I were alone in our bedroom. Our son had stopped living and being less than twenty-four hours ago. The cold April gray had given way to a clear, star-filled sky. We stood together looking out our second-story bedroom window at the magnificent heaven and the warm lights of town in the distance. The world, at least our physical world, seemed so peaceful. In those houses people were laughing, playing, watching television, and sleeping as if nothing of consequence had happened in the world. Didn't they know that humanity had lost a son, a brother, and a fellow traveler who had great potential and many unfulfilled dreams? Clearly the earth and the people in it intended to go on without our Paul. Holding each other, we finally drifted off to a fitful sleep.

CHAPTER THREE
THE DAY AFTER

We both were awake by dawn. The headaches were still there and the tears started anew as we suffered and talked our way through the peculiar circumstances of Paul's death. Others who were up in the house took care of household chores as we contemplated what lay ahead.

Andrew was flying in from Denver and someone had to meet him at the airport. We talked of others we had to call; those whose friendship, love, and support had meant much to us over the years and who would help us, somehow, bear the burden.

We had to meet with the pastor and plan funeral services. We once again had to call on our funeral director friend, this time to pick out a casket—how ghastly that sounds, even now, thirteen years afterward.

We planned to have a reviewal for family and friends, but it would be essentially open to the public. We decided that the reviewal would be on Monday evening and the funeral on Tuesday. These duties involved choices, which were really not important to us but which we made in a perfunctory way and even, in some cases, in a zombie-like state. It was as if reality collided with unreality and left us wedged in the middle and unable to move.

We rarely missed church, but that Sunday we didn't go. We simply didn't remember that it was Sunday. We were too numb to pray, but others prayed for us. I, at least, was not sure what to say to God. Some well-meaning folks tried to comfort us with their version of God's purpose by saying, "God called Paul home," or "God must have wanted him in heaven." Ultimately, I felt like God didn't have anything to do with Paul's death. I thought God, like us, was a witness to an unwanted tragedy and, like us, was hurting deeply for one of His precious young flock.

We met with Jim that morning and picked out an oak casket. We thought Paul, an outdoorsman, would like that. This thought became a recurrent theme—deciding something on the basis of whether Paul would or wouldn't like it. We also planned the funeral service, selected hymns, and picked out clothes for Paul to be buried in. Like many people his age, Paul spent no more time in a suit than he absolutely had to. It didn't seem right that he spend eternity in one. We selected a crew-neck sweater and a pair of matching dress slacks. When we asked about shoes, Jim told us that the dead are not buried wearing shoes but barefoot or with stockings. To this day I don't know why that is true, or if it is universally true.

After picking up Andrew from the airport later that day, the four of us huddled together in Paul's room. It was a room filled with Paul's cherished things—school mementos, athletic awards, and pictures. Even though he had been away at school for nearly two semesters, his smell was there. We caressed his clothing that hung in the closet and wept again when memories came back to us. Probably that hour shared as a family was the most bittersweet. We all felt the crushing weight of our loss and even more of Paul's loss, but we were grateful for being together. We talked of the accident and of what might have been that could never be. It was a time together that we didn't want to end. The phone and the doorbell were still ringing, but we left them to others as we felt the presence of Paul in our midst at that moment.

Martha's parents, Grandma and Grandpa, as we all called them, were a great comfort to us. In their early eighties then, they were both surprisingly agile of mind and spirit. They, too, talked of their many memories of Paul. Indeed, they were at our home babysitting the other two boys when Paul was born. Grandpa had gone on walks with him in the fields behind our house, and together they examined whatever nature had to offer that day—a vacated bird's nest, a startled rabbit, a red-tail hawk soaring overhead. At the end of their treks they would return to our home, where Grandma would have freshly baked cookies waiting. When Paul was slighted or bullied by his older brothers he was comforted by both grandparents, who redirected him or offered him some explanation for the disagreement.

Fatigue and numbness were setting in, but sleep was elusive—at least any meaningful sleep. When the psyche is stressed and one is not at peace, restfulness is nearly impossible. There is, perhaps imprinted in the brain from more primitive times, a need to do something, to take some action. One of the many frustrations of death is that there is nothing to do, or more accurately, to undo. Nothing works to put the mind at rest and there is, therefore, no escape from the torment. The dream world tries to solve the puzzle too.

I remember a vivid dream, or nightmare, in which I was trapped in a pickup truck that was sinking in water. My foot was somehow caught in the door of the truck and I could not free it. When I startled awake in a sweat and with heart pounding, my foot was tangled in the sheets.

Martha reported dreams of Paul, too, and over time we have shared the content of our dreams with each other, sometimes thinking they are visions and perhaps the way Paul can make contact through the spiritual realm. I have many dreams of water now. In fact, most of my dreams involve water in some form—either a lake or stream. Over the last few years the water, murky in earlier dreams, has gotten clearer. If there are fish present, which there often are, they are now brightly colored. If I am standing in the water, which I often am, the water is cool and feels pleasant. I interpret these dreams to somehow mean acceptance of Paul's death and like to think that perhaps he visits them upon me.

That evening the family arrived at the small chapel a few minutes before the reviewal was to begin. Paul was lying in his oak casket at the end of the long, narrow room. Floral arrangements lined the sides of the room and gave the air a heavy sweetness.

There was a table with Paul's memorabilia spread out on it, along with many pictures that purported to tell the story of his short life. With the help of Andrew and Peter, we had tried to select objects that were of importance to Paul. He had been active in sports in high school—especially football and wrestling. In his senior year he had been elected to the all-conference football team, and so there were plaques and newspaper clippings. There were scouting items and church confirmation group pictures. All in all, it was a small but precious gathering of recollections that helped us at that moment to celebrate a short life well lived.

We spent some time together standing by the casket holding hands and wanting so badly for Paul to be included in our living, breathing, and loving group. Soon our last moment of being all together as a family was over as many hundreds of people began to arrive to pay their last respects to Paul and offer kind and supportive words to us. We had placed some notepaper in the chapel lobby and asked Paul's friends and classmates to write their recollections of him and to place them in a box. Many did so, and as we read them over and over days later they were a great comfort to us. They also brought back many vivid memories of Paul's life and more tears as we shared them. We had gotten so used to the weeping occasioned by these moments that we didn't apologize for it or think it unusual in any way. Often one person's recollections and tears would trigger another until we were again in anguish together.

We grew tired as the night wore on, as not only Paul's many friends from both high school and college came, but also my patients, Martha's coworkers from American Airlines, and our many friends from the community and church. There were several couples from The Compassionate Friends who also came and introduced us to the organization, with which we had not been familiar. One couple in particular gave us a book to read and were actually the ones who made the suggestion of the "memory box." These contacts, while graciously offered, were not so important to us at the moment, but would be weeks and months later.

By ten o'clock that night the room was again empty except for family, and we were exhausted and the crying headaches had returned. We said our final goodbyes to Paul, and the casket was closed. We would never see him again, at least not in his present form.

We left the chapel reluctantly and drove home in silence, oblivious to the cold and dark April night.

CHAPTER FOUR
THE FUNERAL

At least the sun was shining. We all arrived at the church a little early, but the pews were already beginning to fill. We were greeted with hugs, tears, and many expressions of love and comfort as we were seated in the family section of the fellowship hall. We waited. "Dog and Butterfly," a popular song at the time, was playing over the speakers. This had been one of Paul's favorites according to his brothers. Like many parents, Martha and I would not necessarily have been aware of this generational information. It was rather mournful and eerie for us to hear it for the first time. As we listened carefully to the words, we thought of Paul and the things that were important to him. Perhaps we also began, then, to think about things in our own lives that were not so very important anymore. Always up on the news, we really didn't care what was going on in the rest of the world .We thought of some of our own problems and the issues with which we were struggling, and they seemed quite insignificant.

We watched the church fill up on closed circuit television, and we could hear murmuring over the speakers as the gathering talked softly among themselves. Paul's casket was now closed and had been wheeled to the front of church in front of the altar. As the church pews filled, the overflow into the fellowship hall began. It was 1:30 in the afternoon as Grandma and Grandpa, Martha and I, Andrew and Peter, Martha's sister, Mary, and her children were ushered into the two front pews of the sanctuary.

The service for the funeral was taken from the Lutheran Book of Worship. Both pastors shared in the message. We sang, "Lift High the Cross." As a little fellow, Paul had reluctantly attended weekly church services, and whenever that particular hymn was sung he clasped his hands together and held them up as if lifting up a cross. We were never sure where he had learned that, but assume it was in Sunday school or one of the church programs. To this day, "Lift High the Cross" brings tears to our eyes. We sang "Children of the Heavenly Father," which seems like it was written (1870) especially for the death of a child.

Though He giveth or He taketh, God, his children, ne'er forsaketh;

His the loving purpose solely, to preserve them pure and Holy.

From all evil things He spares them, in His mighty arms he bears them.

We do not even *try* to sing this hymn any more.

In our pre-funereal counseling with the pastors, we were asked if anyone wanted to speak for the family. Public speaking was not foreign to me; I briefly considered it but wisely knew that I could never get through it. To our surprise, Grandpa, an accomplished storyteller and speaker, agreed to do it. He rose admirably to the occasion, his voice deep and mellow with words richly comforting. The memories of his association with Paul and their many outings together were recounted, as well as the importance of Paul's place in our family and his loving relationship with his brothers. His voice cracked only once, as he fought back tears foretelling how much we would all miss

"Pauly." Fellow mourners would tell us for years afterwards how much they remembered his words and how courageous he was to speak publicly at that time what was in all our hearts. Grandpa went to join Paul two years later when he died suddenly at the age of eighty-three.

As the final words were uttered, we filed out past the many sad faces. The church was indeed filled with many of Paul's friends and classmates. Martha's coworkers, our friends, and my patients had come impressive distances to pay their respects. We were seated in cars lined up behind the hearse as Paul's friends bore his casket to the waiting vehicle.

There was a strong April wind and bright sun as the long line of cars moved slowly to the small and very old cemetery. Headlights were on in spite of the sun. The cemetery was less than a mile from the church. As we turned in the gate and drove down the long, tree-lined lane, I noticed for the first time the brown of the landscape not yet wakened from winter's sleep. It momentarily recalled for me the life-death cycle that is so much a part of our existence and how much we accept, indeed, look forward to, the season changes—except when the cycle involves our own lives and those of our family and friends. I thought then, and still believe, that the pain of losing a child derives in part from the anger we feel that the "natural cycle" of life has been interrupted. We humans, like the rest of living things in nature, are supposed to have a timeline. We are born, we live, and we die. There is something terribly wrong and out of balance when a child dies in the bloom of life. Yet how often it happens.

We parked and walked to the graveside. It had been meticulously prepared and covered with a colorful canopy. I would learn years later that a local man well into retirement age had dug the grave, like all graves in that cemetery, by hand. I chanced to play golf with this person some ten years later and learned how moved he is when he has to dig a grave for a young person, and how he takes pride in his work and sees it as his gift to the family to do it well, sculpted and even.

Martha and I held hands as the Lutheran graveside service progressed and Paul's casket was lowered into the waiting vault.

O God, our Father, your beloved Son took children into his arms and blessed them. Give us grace, we pray, that we may entrust Paul to your never-failing care and love, and bring us all to your heavenly kingdom;

through your Son, Jesus Christ our Lord.

In sure and certain hope of the resurrection to eternal life through our Lord, Jesus Christ, we commend to almighty God our son Paul, and we commit his body to its resting place. We commend our brother and son to the Lord. May the Lord receive him into His peace and raise him up on the last day

Our Father in Heaven...

And so it continued.

A handful of dirt was thrown on the top of the casket and it was over. We returned to our waiting cars for the ride back to the church, where the women of the congregation had prepared a reception and lunch. There were still more than 200 people there, and we spoke with many of them and bore their hugs and words of consolation. There was some chatter and even laughter as people who hadn't seen each other for a while met and renewed their acquaintances. Life was taking over and closing the door on unwanted death.

We stayed at the fellowship hall and felt the loving support of all who shared our angst. Even though we were not at peace, we were being comforted and were hesitant to leave. Eventually the volunteers in the kitchen cleared the dishes away and our fellow mourners said their last goodbyes. We left reluctantly for a dark and empty house. None of us can really recall what happened during the rest of that day. The sun probably set and we had a light supper. The phone didn't ring and no one came to the door. The painful things that had to be done were done, and an indescribable heaviness sat on our collective shoulders. The future was unimaginable; the rest of the week seemed unattainable.

CHAPTER FIVE

THE FINAL GOODBYE

We gathered in the kitchen for coffee Wednesday morning and talked about the rest of the week. We all had jobs and classes to return to eventually, but we had the rest of the week to be together. We agreed that we had to go to Paul's room at the university to collect his things and talk to some of his friends. Tentatively we talked of visiting the scene of the accident, and it seemed like something we all wanted to do. Grandma and Grandpa would stay and tend the house and the phone while Martha, Andrew, Peter, and I would drive to Duluth. Martha and I were both told by our offices to take as much time from work as we needed, but at that point, we didn't have any idea how much time would be "needed." Indeed, needed for what? Crying? Praying? Sleeping? What we needed was not clear to us. We still felt a need to connect somehow with Paul; returning to his room and the scene of his death would somehow give us that opportunity.

The four of us headed up the highway in silence, each wondering what we would see and hear that might ease our burden. We found Paul's off-campus room and were let in by one of his housemates. His room was fairly neat. Some books and unfinished papers were on the desk. We saw pictures of all of us as well as some athletic trophies and high school mementos about the room. Everything we saw and touched brought new tears, but as we sat and talked in his room we felt a closeness to Paul that made us feel that his spirit was in the room with us. We savored this felt presence as we carefully gathered his things and packed them in the car. We found the portable fish house which Paul and I had built together and which he'd never had a chance to use. His ambitious plans for ice fishing evidently never got in the way of his studies.

Later that evening a young man and fellow student came to our motel room. He was Paul's commanding officer in

ROTC. Most graciously, he shared with us Paul's plan to be a pilot in the Air Force. He told us of Paul's dedication to flight and to the ROTC program. We had seen evidence of Paul's growth and maturity during his freshman year, but it was good to hear it from a fellow student who'd sought us out to confirm what we believed.

The next morning we called the county sheriff and asked if we could visit with him and see the accident site. He was courteous and welcoming, as he had been on the phone when he'd called the previous Saturday morning with the life-changing news.

Later, we all sat around a table in his office while the sheriff recounted for us the details of the accident investigation. His report confirmed what we had learned from Greg, the boy who had survived. We saw pictures of the car being pulled from the creek and of Paul's body lying lifeless across the back seat. At first, the sheriff was hesitant to show us these graphic pictures, but I went around the table and asked everyone if they wanted to see them. We all did. Although vivid, they were not difficult for us to view; in fact, they brought us one step closer to the last moment when Paul had been a living, breathing part of our lives. We thanked the sheriff. As we were leaving, the parents of Eric, the driver of the car, who also drowned, were waiting to see the sheriff, too. I was struck by this coincidence: that both families had the same need—to visit the scene of the accident and know the details. Although "closure" was not a word we were familiar with at that time, we would later view this visit as an important step in our acceptance of Paul's death. We talked briefly with Eric's parents, whom we had not met. It turned out that Eric was their only child, and so they had no other family members with whom to share their sorrow. It was hard to see ourselves as fortunate, but we at least had two other children. Then, as now, we took consolation where we could find it.

We went to the salvage yard where the car in which the boys had been riding was now resting. How innocuous it looked in innocent repose, this chamber of death that only days before had claimed two young lives. It was a two-door hardtop, which meant that Paul had had virtually no chance of escaping from the back seat once the car was overturned in water. We were surprised how little damage there was. The passenger door was dented and could not be opened. We were amazed that Greg had gotten out (he didn't remember how) and Eric, the driver, had not. The left rear window was broken; Paul had evidently broken it with a hockey stick but could not fit through the narrow window as the dark, cold water poured into the car. We all stood shaken and silent as we imagined his final moments of struggle. Again we felt Paul's spirit nearby.

Our final stop was one we dreaded most and yet felt drawn to: the small creek where the accident happened. As it came into view, we could hardly believe that now, five days later, no longer full of snow runoff, it had nearly returned to its normal size. It could not even contain an automobile now, much less completely submerge one. We studied the curve in the road and the culvert that had brought the skidding car to an abrupt halt but failed to keep it from turning on its back in the creek as the momentum of the vehicle overwhelmed it. Again we were silent as we each imagined the accident and the conversations that the boys must have had as their predicament dawned on them and the weakening ice began to give way. We stood on the roadside, gazing into the now calmer water. I believe it was there we said our final goodbyes to our son and brother.

CHAPTER SIX
THE JOURNEY BACK

At home again, we knew the impossible had to happen. In one sense our lives had to return to some form of normalcy, and yet they would never be the same. Andrew spent a day with Peter at college and the rest of the week with us at home before leaving for Colorado. Peter had to return to college to finish his senior year and make plans for his future. Grandma and Grandpa, though in their eighties, had schedules and responsibilities. None of us felt "normal" and could not, in fact, imagine getting back into a routine. Time becomes the enforcer, however, and eventually we said our lingering and painful goodbyes, knowing that phone calls and letters would have to bind us until we could be together again. Grandpa had always been a disciplined letter writer. In our twenty-seven year marriage we had probably averaged a letter a week from him. Typewritten and newsy, they contained many words of wisdom and support that would help sustain us in the months ahead.

Alone, Martha and I faced yet another difficult decision. Monday was bearing down on us and we had to decide whether to return to our jobs. Martha, in her work for the airlines, interacted with the public all day long. Although her coworkers had been very supportive and comforting to us both during the past week, the harried air travelers would not know of her ache just beneath the surface. She would indeed have to put on a "happy face."

By contrast, nearly all of my patients knew of our family tragedy, and most had known Paul personally. How would they and I resume our professional relationship? Would they be comfortable telling me of their physical complaints, worries, and concerns, knowing the dark cloud that hung over my head? It seemed at the time like the "elephant in the room" that no one would want to talk about.

As we considered the alternatives and options, there did not seem to be any good ones. Yes, we could take more time off.

We could visit our children. We could revisit the site of the accident. We could visit and decorate Paul's grave. We could, in effect, extend the acute grieving process and make a career out of it. We would learn later of a teacher who had lost a child and who took an extended leave of absence visiting schools and planting a tree at each in memory of his son. That approach did not appeal to us. Nor were we anxious to become immersed in the workaday world with its schedules, challenges, and long hours. No one would think less of us if we took an extra week or even a month for ourselves, but, in truth, we were fearful of wallowing in self-pity. Self is the key word here. Yes, we were in pain, but we were alive. It was Paul who had lost the chance at life, and our tears and heartaches were for him. We knew by instinct or experience that at some point our grieving could turn inward and turn sadness into depression. We ourselves would then, in effect, become the objects of our own mourning, and somehow that would detract from Paul's life and death. In the end we decided to try work.

For us it turned out to be the right decision. Martha's interaction with passengers demanded her full attention and concentration. They did not know or care of her personal loss.

During these times she mustered her will and felt briefly "normal." She grew in her personal strength and reaffirmed her own selfhood, and at the end of each day she knew that her suffering, while great, would not consume her. Her coworkers, of course, knew her pain and surrounded her and protected her when she needed it. They were a constant source of energy and support for her.

Likewise my patients, colleagues, and staff carried me. Initial patient visits were often tearful as we talked briefly of the "elephant in the room." Typically a patient would offer an expression of comfort such as, "How are *you* doing?" I would thank them and say something like, "It's tough, but we're okay." It wasn't exactly true, of course. We weren't okay, but a more complex discussion did not seem in order. Sometimes other things happened. Once when I had just returned to the office, a woman who had been my patient for a long time, virtually leaped off the exam table and threw her arms about me. It was too much and we both had a good cry. Sometime later we shared a laugh when we recalled that she had only been wearing a flimsy exam gown. After these initial words I was better able to get down to business; in fact, I like to think I was attentive to patient's problems with a renewed sensitivity. A feeling that I can best describe as raw reality was my companion in those early days. It was also the beginning of change in my attitudes toward death. Both my patients and my own mortality took on new meaning.

And so we made it through those first days, and weeks turned into months, and months turned into a year. We talked to our kids and Grandpa and Grandma frequently as others stopped talking about it. But mostly we got up in the morning, often after a restless and dream-filled sleep, and put one foot ahead of the other and got through each day doing our duties. We didn't get much stronger but we didn't lose ground either. We shared "Paul memories" with each other and with the family. Sometimes while sitting at night in front of the fireplace, one of us would have a vivid recollection of Paul's face, or of him coming down the steps, or ways he had of speaking that we would share, sometimes in sadness, but often thankful for these visitations of memory that ever-so-briefly brought him back to us.

There are many euphemisms for this behavior after the death of a loved one. Some call it *coping*. Still others say, *handling it* or *getting through it. Dealing with it* or *adjusting to it*, are two more. There are others. I don't find any of these descriptions very accurate or comforting. We do what we have to do depending on who we are, while "it" handles us. The death of a child takes you on a journey like a hawk carries a rabbit through the sky. It eventually drops you either dead or wounded. What you see and do on the journey is up to you. The journey itself is not.

CHAPTER SEVEN

LIVING
HOLLOW

One year later...

Martha and I were functioning, but we weren't really living. There was little joy, and effort was needed to take satisfaction in so-called simple pleasures. The mental health professionals have a name for this mental state. They call it anhedonia—the inability to get pleasure from life. There is another high-class word that describes our state then—anergic. We had no energy.

We came home from our work to a cold and empty house, and the full impact of the "empty nest" hit us. The winter that first year seemed colder and longer. Normally we are both winter people. We enjoy the sense of excitement that accompanies a winter storm and the warmth of a cozy fire while the snow and wind rage outside. A cup of tea, listening to music, watching the Vikings play on Sunday after church were all things we had previously looked forward to. Although we still did those things, they seemed to require more energy and were not as satisfying.

I don't remember how long it was after Paul's death until we laughed again, nor do I remember what it was we laughed at. But I do remember it didn't feel right. We felt somehow guilty, I remember. How strange it seemed that there should be any humor in the world or a smile on anyone's lips. Gradually we realized that the rest of the world was moving on. Other things were happening as usual, both good and not so good. Babies were being born. Other people were dying. Sometimes the youthful were prematurely snatched from their parents just like Paul had been. It became clear that the world was going to go forward and our heavy hearts were not going to hold it back.

Like other forms of pleasure, intimacy was hard for us. We shared our sorrow together, but our infrequent pleasures came to us at different times. When I had a good day at the office and the gloom lifted for a day or two, Martha would be down. And if she was moving out of her despair, I could drag her back with a word or a glance or even just an unarticulated mood that she could sense. It seemed that we were never in the same place with it at the same time. We would fall asleep watching the late evening news and bed seemed like the only escape.

There were physiological changes as well as psychological ones. Although fifty-one and on the threshold of menopause at the time of Paul's death, Martha had not experienced any signs or symptoms of that female milestone. Within one month, she began having night sweats and hot flashes so uncomfortable that she had to be put on estrogen and never had a physiological menses again. We both lost weight, had little interest in food, and had accelerated graying of our hair.

During this time of "walking in the valley of the shadow of death," it was difficult for our friends to support us. They would have been glad, for the most part, to talk with us about Paul and in some cases did so, but were understandably afraid to bring him up on their own. Curiously, it must have seemed to them that to mention his death would remind us of something we had forgotten. Nothing could have been further from the truth.

He was on our minds constantly that first year. If his name was mentioned and our eyes moistened, people must have thought they caused the tears and so were reluctant to do it again. Often friends would ask, "How are you doing?" and this would give us the opportunity to discuss how we were feeling at the moment. Occasionally we chose not to revisit the pain and simply said "okay," and changed the subject.

Also, during this time, we discovered we are not grave tenders. Paul is buried in a beautifully wooded cemetery. He is in the new section where the markers are flat to allow for mowing, but each has a hole for a post to support a pot of flowers. With the help of Andrew and Peter, we picked out a simple granite marker with Paul's name and dates of birth and death on it. There is a carving of a golden retriever, a butterfly, and a small cross in each corner. At the bottom it says, simply, "Son of Robert and Martha. Brother of Andrew and Peter." In the spring we plant flowers in the pot, which requires us to visit once a week or so in the dry season to water them. At Christmas we pick out a small fir tree and decorate it with red ribbons. This seems right to us as we recall how much Paul loved holidays, especially Christmas. Yet, for all foregoing, we really don't get a lot of solace out of visiting the grave site, as it appears some do. We see many of the same people at the cemetery each time we are there, and many graves have elaborate floral displays, signs, dream catchers, and the like. We stand briefly and stare down at the grave, and suppose that in these moments we are closer to what was Paul, physically, than at any other time. Yet there are no great moments or spiritual insights at these times, and as hard as we listen, he does not have any messages for us.

In the span of a year we had reached the bottom of our desolation, and healing began.

PART TWO

SUPPORT AND HEALING

Ah, my little Barney, you have gone to follow a new stream,

clear as crystal, flowing through fields of wonderful flowers that never fade.

It is a strange river to Teddy and me; strange and very far away.

Someday we shall see it with you; and you will teach us the names

of those blossoms that do not wither. But 'till then, little Barney,

the other lad and I will follow the old stream

that flows by the woodland fireplace—your altar.

Rue grows here. Yes, there is plenty of rue. But there is also rosemary,

that's for remembrance! And close beside it I see a little heart's ease.

HENRY VAN DYKE (WRITING ON THE DEATH OF HIS SON)

CHAPTER EIGHT

SUPPORT

In grief nothing stays put. One keeps emerging from a phase, but it always recurs. Round and round. Everything repeats. Am I going in circles, or dare I hope I am on a spiral? Grief is like a long valley, a winding valley where any bend may reveal a totally new landscape.

C. S. LEWIS, AFTER THE DEATH OF HIS WIFE.

Support is one of those oft-used words, the meaning of which seems obvious and universally understood. In reality, its meaning is different for each person, and we each derive support in different ways. That is also why it is hard to give unless and until we take time to discern what a particular person needs and wants.

For example, some who are grieving like to be touched and even held; others prefer verbal support, perhaps in the form of openness and a willingness to linger and talk about their loved ones. Timing is also important. There were times when we wanted to talk about Paul and other times when our vulnerability told us we didn't want to.

It is in that sense that the following suggestions are offered for those who grieve a child's loss. These are thoughts and support systems that we found helpful through our journey.

Most things help a little, while nothing takes all the pain away. Healing—and by healing I mean the formation of a scar—is incremental, not apocalyptic. It occurs in small ways and over time—who is to say how much time? For us there was no good "end point." We never actually knew when we were there and when the scar was complete, for it would break open anew and start again. Even though we were able to return to a normal and pleasurable life, hardly a day passes that we do not remember Paul. Sometimes it is a thought recalled by old photographs, a song, or simply a word from an old friend that provides a fleeting image of him as a baby, a blond preschooler, or the mature young man he became. Now, far from avoiding these memories, we look forward to and cherish them.

What follows are points of light that led us on our journey of healing.

CHAPTER NINE

CHURCH AND
FAMILY

The old World War I expression "There are no atheists in foxholes" comes readily to mind. I don't think many who have lost a child are true atheists. If one belongs to an organized religion, so much the better, but many who suffer do not. It is not my intention to suggest that everyone who loses a child join a church or start reading the Bible, Torah, or Quran, but I believe at some point in their acute loss, most people will turn to their concept of God in despair and hopelessness to seek an answer or, at least, comfort. I also believe that God hears their prayers and does provide comfort. For us, it came in the form of our Lutheran faith.

We had always attended church and became regular members of our present congregation when we moved to town nearly thirty years ago. Our church became a source of great comfort when tragedy befell us. Some say they find God while walking quietly through the woods on a sunny fall day. Others say they find God on the golf course or fishing on a calm lake early in the morning. When Paul died, we could not find God in those places. We found Him in the fellowship of our congregation. Church members came to our house, brought us food, sent us cards and letters, and prayed for us. It was their attention and concern that felt "supportive" to us and which we still feel fourteen years later. Also, in those fourteen years others in our community, and in our congregation, have lost children, and we have tried to help them in similar ways. This principle of grieving parents helping other grieving parents is, I believe, a valid therapeutic principle, and one which is an important aspect of The Compassionate Friends (see Chapter 11).

Although the grief parents feel is unique to them, others in the family suffer a great loss and experience it in different ways, depending on their relationships to the lost child.

Grandparents feel a unique sense of loss, not only for the grandchild, but for *their* children whom they see suffering. Perhaps, because of their age, they view death in a different way, and while it may hold shock, it probably does not have the same mystery for them that it does their grown children. Both my and Martha's parents suffered our loss with us and were a source of comfort to us. They also worried about us and our other children as they watched our struggle take place over time and in different ways.

Siblings, likewise, experience death and grieving in unique ways determined in part by their ages and the closeness of their relationships to the lost child. It is possible for them to experience "survivor guilt" and wonder why their brother or sister was taken and not them. The 1970s movie, *Ordinary People* deals with this theme. This film illustrates well the stress and havoc that the death of a child can wreak on family relationships when not dealt with in a healing way. Each sibling has a different relationship with the lost one, and, like each adult, heals at a different time and in a different way. There is no timetable for grief. As Louise Erdrich says in her book *The Last Report on the Miracles at Little No Horse*, "Grief has its own rules and power."

In our case, Andrew and Peter were young adults, were out of the home, and were beginning to engage in their chosen life's work. It was important for us to keep in touch with them, which we did often by phone and frequent visits.

At the first anniversary of Paul's death, we tried to be all together as a family. Andrew, in Colorado, could not be with us, but Peter and Martha's parents joined us for a memorial service in our home. We lit a candle for Paul and shared memories of him as well as some readings. It was during this time we appreciated the "letters of memory" that Paul's classmates had written and left with us at the funeral. This gathering was a tearful and painful undertaking, but I believe, in retrospect, that it was a milestone in our healing process.

One of our fears was that we would forget Paul. Forget his voice, his mannerisms, and even how he looked. By sharing stories and memories as well as viewing pictures and old videos, we have kept more vivid recollections in our hearts and minds.

Finally emptying Paul's room at home was, likewise, a painful process which I think is the reason many grieving parents leave the room untouched, "as he left it." It serves not so much as a "shrine" to the lost one as a place to recapture some of the old familiar sights and even smells. It was several years before we could bear to give away some of Paul's clothes, toys, or other memorabilia. We only recently gave his saxophone to a childhood friend and close friend of the family who, in his adult years, decided to play the sax. It gave us comfort and pleasure to see Paul's memory kept alive in this way. We still have some of his clothes and other keepsakes, which we will always have and hold onto as a way of preserving memories.

Similarly, Martha kept the Easter eggs Paul colored when he was home for the final time. She keeps them in the back of the refrigerator and, surprisingly, they have maintained their color and shape all these years!

CHAPTER TEN

THE HEALING FUNERAL

Denying sadness denies healing.

By letting your heart break

You let your heart heal

GALE MASSEY, M.S.

The funeral of one's child is surely one of the most devastating, heart-bursting experiences that anyone can imagine. It was so for us, as I've indicated in earlier chapters. If you're reading this book, it's likely that you too have been through such a tormenting process for your child, sibling, or someone you know. Paradoxically, I believe, the funeral and reviewal also present the first opportunity for some healing of the wound that will never go away.

When I was a young intern working in a pediatric emergency room, I had an experience that left an indelible impression on me. A four-year-old child was brought in by ambulance after being hit by a car. He had run out between two parked cars and in an instant his life was ended. Resuscitative efforts were to no avail in the emergency room. We were all feeling helpless and sad as we covered his limp but unmarked body with a sheet and placed it in a private, out-of-the-way examination room, awaiting the parents. The charge nurse asked me if I would greet the parents and tell them the devastating news, and I agreed to do so. Only the father came, and I nervously ushered him into a private office and told him that in spite of our efforts, his son had been fatally injured. I was relieved that he took it relatively well. He asked for details and circumstances, and I shared these with him as best I could. He sat holding his head in his hands for a few minutes and then asked quietly if he could see his son. I looked at the experienced nurse and she nodded. Then we escorted the father to the room where his tiny four-year-old lay on the gurney, covered with a sheet. As he uncovered his son he began a mournful howl that eventually dissolved in tears. He held his son and sobbed for the better part of an hour while I stood uncomfortably by, trying to console him in a "professional" way. I'm not sure the father was even aware of my presence. As uncomfortable as it was for a novice physician having no experience in these matters, I knew that something important was taking place that could not have taken place if the father had not seen his son. There would always have been an element of disbelief and denial that would have persisted and not permitted healing to take place. Little did I realize at the time that I would eventually have to live through this agonizing event several times in my professional life and, finally, with one of my own children.

I am not suggesting that viewing the body is a public event or that it *should* be done by anyone other than the immediate family, or even that it should be done in all cases. I do believe that it confirms in an important way what eventually will have to be accepted by all the family—the immutability and finality of the tragedy. I can only wonder at the horror of those families whose children disappear, never to be seen or heard from again. The difference between disappearance and never "knowing for sure," and confirming death by one's own senses, is hope. As long as there is hope that death did not take place there cannot be closure and healing. Acceptance of the death sets the stage for healing of the heart.

The funeral, by contrast, *is* a public event. Indeed, in most cases, funerals are open to the public so that others may share the acute pain of the loss with the family, and to offer their support, bid their farewell, and honor the memory of the lost child. In our case, hundreds of people came to Paul's funeral, some from long distances. We felt honored and supported by their efforts and we felt that their presence honored Paul as well. But mainly, they just helped us walk through it physically, emotionally, and spiritually, and we can't imagine the hell it would have been without them. They shared stories about Paul with us that we hadn't known and helped us appreciate him even more. This was especially true of his classmates and friends, who were obviously shocked and felt a great sense of loss. Their presence was a real comfort to us, and as mentioned earlier, their written memories of Paul continue to support us as we reread them years later.

To acknowledge the support we received from the church, community, and friends, as well as those who came to Paul's funeral we sent out cards with the following message, which is just as heartfelt today as it was then:

Dear Friends,

With the sudden and tragic loss of our son and brother, Paul, we have felt the most acute pain that any of us have ever known. Without your help and comfort we don't see how we could have gotten through it. We feel that you literally put your collective arms around us and helped us stand. To those of you who called, came to the house, came to the visitation and funeral, and to those many of you who sent flowers, brought food, and gave memorials and cards, a mere "thank you" will never be enough. We love you, and please know how much your broad shoulders helped us bear the burden of our grief.

Although the pain for us is very great right now and we miss Paul very much, as we know many of you do, too, we see in his untimely death multiple reasons for celebrating life and continuing to grow spiritually. We hope you, too, will use his death as a means to renew your faith in the cycle of life and death and resurrection that is God's plan.

BOB, MARTHA, ANDREW, AND PETER

CHAPTER ELEVEN

THE
COMPASSIONATE
FRIENDS

The Compassionate Friends Credo

We need not walk alone.

We are The Compassionate Friends.

We reach out to each other with love, understanding,

and with hope.

Our children have died at all ages and from many

different causes,

But our love for our children unites us.

Your pain becomes my pain, just as your hope

becomes my hope.

We come together from all walks of life, from many

different circumstances.

We are a unique family because we represent

many races and creeds.

We are young and we are old.

Some of us are far along in our grief, but others still

feel a grief so fresh and so intensely painful that

we feel helpless and see no hope.

Some of us have found our faith

to be a source of strength;

Some of us are struggling to find answers.

Some of us are angry, filled with guilt,

or in deep depression.

Others radiate an inner peace.

But whatever pain we bring to this gathering of

The Compassionate Friends, it is pain we will share

just as we share with each other our love

for our children.

We are all seeking and struggling to build a future for

ourselves, but we are committed to building a future

together as we reach out to each other in love

And share the pain as well as the joy,

Share the anger as well as the peace,

Share the faith as well as the doubts,

And help each other to grieve as well as to grow.

We need not walk alone.

We are The Compassionate Friends.

Sometime during that first year after Paul's death, we got a call from a local woman about The Compassionate Friends. Alice and Mike had lost a son of the same age about five years before. When Paul died, Alice came by the house and dropped off the book *Goodbye My Son, Hello* by Adolpho Quezada. It is a painful book to read, but lovely in its message and as comforting to us as anything could have been during that time. The book was not related to The Compassionate Friends, but it was Alice who contacted us later and told us that she and her husband were getting a group together to share their grief experiences. She told us then about the national organization, The Compassionate Friends, specifically founded to support grieving parents and siblings who had lost a child.

We cautiously attended our first meeting where we met five or six other couples or, in some cases, a single parent. After reciting the Credo, we introduced ourselves and shared our stories to the extent that we were comfortable doing so. The stories were in many ways similar. The circumstances of each child's death were different, but most were accidental deaths involving automobiles. There was one couple who lost a daughter to leukemia and a mother whose son committed suicide during his first year of college. Our eyes moistened afresh as each person told of the phone call or policeman's visit that announced the tragedy. The shock, disbelief, and gloom that followed was acutely familiar to all of us, and we nodded silently in affirmation as each person told his or her story.

The meetings were not all tears and sadness. On the occasion of a child's birthday we would light a candle and tell stories, sometimes humorous, of the child's life and of happier times together. Through this process we gradually came to celebrate Paul's birthdate more than to grieve his death date. In fact, we now remember him by placing flowers on our church's altar not on the date he was killed, but on the date of his birth.

Compassionate Friends was therapeutic and healing for us. It was not difficult to recount Paul's life and death in that setting as we attended monthly meetings over a period of a year or more. The group welcomed new members, mostly parents, sometimes siblings, but stayed about the same size— ten to twelve persons at each meeting—as people drifted in and out.

We came to believe through our experience with this group that grief shared by many is grief borne by many. Through our time with The Compassionate Friends, we drew strength from helping new members walk the walk that none of us chose, and by so doing, the dark cloud that would always hang over our heads came to interfere in our daily lives less and less. Although it would never become a friend, the cloud gave us a sensitivity to the pain and suffering of others that I do not believe we could have acquired in any other way.

Since then we have been called on a few times to talk to parents whose child has just been taken. I like to think we offer some measure of comfort, but it always seems less than enough. No single person can do this comforting. It comes from many and over a long period of time.

There is a teaching in the Jewish faith that is also reflected in an African proverb: "Sticks in a bundle are unbreakable, but sticks alone can be broken by a child."

We can, and do, empathize with grieving parents as best we can, and sometime later we refer them to The Compassionate Friends meetings.

(See page 99 for the address and web site of The Compassionate Friends)

CHAPTER TWELVE

MENTAL HEALTH ISSUES

In the Sixties, when an unexpected death occurred in the family, hospitals and medication were not far away. I know this to be the case because I was a resident in a metropolitan hospital at that time. It was not unusual to offer medication to family members who had just lost a child or a sibling. In a spirit of trying to be helpful, nurses and doctors would come with a little "med cup" containing a single dose of Valium or Librium for the bereaved. It was not considered professional to embrace or hug or weep with parents. I think medication was all we thought we could do. In some cases even powerful antipsychotic drugs were offered and, like the tranquilizers, readily taken. After all, "the doctors knew best."

It turns out such "helpfulness" was the worst thing to do. Parents who have just lost a child do not need medication—they need physical and emotional support and other forms of help. Putting them in touch with important resources such as their pastor or priest, or helping them to notify friends and relatives or otherwise deal with the overwhelming complexities of death is, of course, what is needed, not tranquilization! Today it is considered acceptable for the health professional to register shock and emotion appropriate to the situation, and there is nothing unprofessional about empathizing with a person or family by touch or embrace.

Dr. Maurice Barry, in a milestone article published in the early Seventies, described a delayed grief response.[1] Dr. Barry, a psychiatrist at the Mayo Clinic, described the case of a severely depressed adult, who, as a child, had seen both parents killed traumatically, and who had not been allowed by family members or relatives to express emotion or grieve openly. This repression of the grief response lay dormant in the subject for nearly thirty years, until serious clinical depression forced him to seek psychiatric help. In the initial stages of therapy, the patient did

[1] MJ Barry Jr., "The Prolonged Grief Reaction," *Mayo Clinic Proceedings* 48 (1973): 329-335.

not mention to the therapist the facts surrounding his parents death. It was only after several sessions, when the therapist became curious and asked about his parents, that the patient described the horrible scene that he had witnessed. The therapist was startled and reacted with an empathetic, "Oh my God! You poor child!" It was then that the patient vaulted from his chair and lay on the floor weeping like a child! He was, in fact, truly experiencing the emotion of acute grief for the first time—thirty years later! It was the beginning of the cure for his depression.

It is not uncommon to encounter patients with depression, as well as chronic, unrelenting medical problems, whose acute grief has been deflected or aborted by medication or well-meaning professionals or family members. These unfortunate and miserable people have little or no recollection of the circumstance surrounding the death of a loved one or their own response to it. These delayed or unresolved grief responses, of course, give their owners no peace and will torment them in one form or another until they eventually relive the traumatic death of the loved one by seeking help through therapy or other means to find resolution.

This is not to say that the death of a child or sibling cannot, by itself, lead to serious clinical depression. It can. When sadness overwhelms, or physical symptoms persist, help should be sought from a mental health professional. Sleeplessness, weight loss, apathy, and difficulty concentrating all are common in the early stages of grieving, in spite of sharing and talking about the death of a loved one. These serious symptoms may continue, however, and result in a persistent melancholia and a form of "involutional" depression that requires medication or perhaps even hospitalization. Those who live with or associate with someone who has experienced the tragic loss of a child, spouse, or sibling should be aware of the potential for this treatable form of depression and, gently urge a person showing symptoms of it to seek treatment or other forms of intervention, as one would for any other form of illness.

Finally, the death of a child can cause serious difficulties in a marriage or other family relationships. Guilt, depression, and inability to get pleasure from simple things in life can rob a marriage of its vitality and make one or both partners blame the other for their circumstance. Statistics show that fully eighty percent of marriages will have some serious disruption, either divorce or separation, after the loss of a child. On a scale of stressful life events, the death of a child is *highest* on the scale.

A contributing factor to spousal dissatisfaction is the fact that we all heal at different rates. It is nearly impossible for both parents to be in the same place at the same time in their feelings toward the lost child and what that means to their lives in general. Laughter or lightheartedness in one spouse can provoke a hurtful and resentful reaction in the other, who may have experienced a particularly bad day in their recollections and not be ready for their partner's mirth.

Some partners are more verbal than others. One mother whose daughter was killed in an accident told me she could not stop talking about it for months afterward to anyone who would listen. By contrast, her husband would *not* talk about it and, although suffering the loss equally, internalized his feelings.

The common ground for the marriage becomes the shared experience of the lost child. The problem, then, is how that experience is "lived" to provide a basis for continued growth in the marriage relationship. Intimacy and emotional closeness, difficult under the best of circumstances, are nearly impossible if resentments, rather than understanding, are nurtured.

I believe that sharing of feelings in a group setting is extremely helpful in counteracting this tendency for marriage partners to drift apart. One of the reasons The Compassionate Friends has been so successful, in my opinion, is that it provides a forum for parents to openly share what they are thinking and feeling at the moment, and for their partners to see that their own thoughts and feelings do not necessarily resonate on the same frequency. A mutually supportive respect for each other's personal grief can, I believe, result in a stronger marriage—one in which both partners rely on each other for mutual support and encouragement, as well as continued personal growth.

CHAPTER THIRTEEN
ACCEPTANCE

Acceptance of Paul's death was not something that occurred for us at a given point in time. Rather it was incremental *over* time. There will be issues of Paul's life and death that will never be resolved for us, and we have accepted that as well. A word, a picture, a song, or a random thought can all trigger pain and memories, and we have accepted those memories as our connection with Paul—a connection that we don't want to lose. In that sense, we don't want to "move on" or "get on with our lives" which imply leaving Paul behind. Instead, these moments have been integrated *into* our daily lives and we welcome them, even cherish them.

No words express acceptance and integration better or more beautifully than those written by Adolfo Quezada as the last entry in the daily journal that he kept after the death of his son, Roberto, and published in his 1985 book, *Goodbye My Son, Hello*.

I haven't written for several days. I'm not sure why. It must have something to do with my not having anything to say. Even today, I begin writing this without having any clear or definite thoughts or feelings.

A deeply tragic yet hopeful realization has overcome me, Roberto. My mind has run out of words that will express myself to you. My feelings, still within me, will be integrated with all of my life and not only with one aspect of it.

Quite simply, I will no longer dwell on your death. Instead, I will remember your life, and what a great part of my life you will always be.

Our relationship, Roberto, has changed. You no longer are of me; rather, I am of you. You are no longer someone whom I must hold onto; you are part of the palm that holds me.

You have gone beyond the reach of my senses only to return at the core of my being. Now we will be together forever and ever.

Goodbye my son, hello.

Perhaps in some philosophical or existential way acceptance also means that we have accepted our *own* mortality. This observation is based on a feeling Martha and I have toward our own death.

Although I have never believed in the mythological heaven that is often portrayed as angels on clouds in white gowns playing harps, I do believe in the eternal and inextinguishable spirit that lives within each of us, and which we call eternal life. While most of us have this hope, Paul's death created a more imminent curiosity and excitement about our own death and reunification with him that outweighs our fear of the final sleep. Without actually looking forward to our own passing, we at least anticipate that Paul will be on the other side to greet us— and what a joyful reunion it will be!

And so, we continue to live our lives, as we're sure Paul would want us to do. We love what is good in the world and are saddened by that which is bad. We enjoy our work, friends, time at the lake, good music, and each other. When possible, we try to be helpful to those who have lost loved ones and to share our experience with them. Though we still grieve we have not become "professional grievers." And most importantly, we love to share stories about Paul's life within the family and also with those outside of the family who ask and express an interest.

In that first spring shortly after Paul died, some dear friends gave us a tree to plant in his memory. It is a lovely green spire linden. In the thirteen years since Paul's death, it has grown into a tall straight tree with large shiny leaves that shade our window. When it blooms in the spring we are reminded of the cycle of life and death that is our very essence as part of humankind. It serves to remind us of that part of Paul that we will always carry in our hearts until our souls meet again.

PART THREE

SOME PEACEFUL MEMORIES

When death strikes down the innocent and young,

for every fragile form from which he lets the panting spirit free,

a hundred virtues rise, in shapes of mercy, charity,

and love, to walk the world and bless it.

Of every tear that sorrowing mortals shed on such green graves

some good is born, some gentler natures comes.

In the Destroyer's steps there spring up

bright creations that defy his power,

and his dark path becomes a way of light to heaven.

CHARLES DICKENS

MEDITATIVE GROUP EXERCISE
Letting Go...A Mourning Walk

The following was a meditative group exercise written by the author and used at The Compassionate Friends. The exercise was conducted by candlelight with a soft musical background while the leader softly and slowly read these words, pausing frequently.

A moment for gathering. Focus on breathing, and relaxation...Listen to the music.

See yourself on a country road. The road leads to a wood, its fall colors illuminated by the soft sunlight...The air is cool, but the sun is warm. It is morning...you start to walk slowly. You are walking down the road and feel good...feel at peace..relaxed..seeing the colors of the trees...the sun warms you through your clothing.

You pass a field of wildflowers...you turn and face them, seeing them move gently in the morning breeze. As you watch them you are aware of your lost loved one standing beside you. You smile and he/she smiles...tears of joy come to your eyes. You do not speak but are aware of each other and begin to walk down the road together. You look at him and he smiles at you...you are aware of his presence...how he feels, how he is dressed. You keep walking slowly down the road. You do not speak but are comfortable and serene in each other's presence.

You see a lake in the distance. The road leads to the lake. The sun is shining on the water and makes diamonds glisten on the surface. The waves are lapping gently at the sandy beach. As you approach the lake you come to four wooden steps that lead to the beach. You pause together at the top step. You are going to start going down the steps slowly. You step down onto the second step. You both look up and see the seagulls gliding overhead. You hear them calling. You step on the third step..then the fourth. Now you are standing on the sand. You have no shoes and the sand feels warm and moist on your feet. You turn and start walking down the sandy beach, listening to the waves gently lapping and hearing the seagulls. You walk together peacefully along the shore...you are content...happy. In the distance ahead you see a silver basket...it is surrounded by an intense white light. It is beautiful and you walk toward it. As you approach the basket you realize it is empty.

You begin to place your worries, cares, and concerns in the basket. You find a tension or a conflict...you look at it and show it to your loved one. He nods and you place it in the basket. Resentments, hurts, and pains you have known go into the basket. You let go of disagreeable feelings and energies you feel toward people or a certain person and put them in the basket. As the basket becomes full it begins to rise. It ascends slowly to the clear blue sky...you and your loved one watch it get smaller and smaller until it becomes a speck and then disappears.

You turn and look at each other and it is time to say goodbye...you touch his hand one more time and he begins to walk down the beach alone. He looks back, waves and smiles. You smile and wave back. Like the basket he gets smaller and smaller and finally disappears down the beach..around the corner. You turn and walk back toward the stairs. You feel relaxed and happy. You walk up the stairs slowly. The first one...the second one...pause on the third step and then again on the top. You turn and look back at the lake one more time. Its top shimmers in the light...the air is warm...you hear the seagulls...

You start to walk slowly down the road into the fall colors. You pause at the wildflowers and admire their softness and beauty...you complete your walk.

You feel happy that you can return to this place and walk along this road and along the lake with your loved one whenever you want. This is your own special place and you can come here as often as you like.

Now open your eyes and feel relaxed and calm...

I'M FREE

Don't grieve for me for now I'm free
I'm following the path God has laid you see.
I took His hand when I heard his call
I turned my back and left it all.

I could not stay another day
To laugh, to love, to work or play
Tasks left undone must stay that way
I found the peace at the close of day.

If my parting has left a void
Then fill it with remembered joys—
A friendship shared, a laugh, a kiss
Oh yes, these things I too will miss.

Be not burdened with times of sorrow.
I wish you the sunshine of tomorrow.
My life's been full, I savored much,
Good friends, good times, a loved one's touch.

Perhaps my time seemed all too brief—
Don't lengthen it now with undue grief.
Lift up your hearts, and peace to thee—
God wanted me now; He set me free.

AUTHOR UNKNOWN

FOR ALL WHO MOURN

By Arthur Guiterman

That he was near to you
So many a year
But darkens your distress.
Would you he were
Less worthy and less dear
That you might grieve the less?

He was a golden font
That freely poured
What goldenly endures,
And though that font be gone,
Its bounty stored
And treasured,
Still is yours.

The past is deathless.
Souls are wells too deep
To spend their purest gains.
All that he gave to you
Is yours to keep
While memory remains.

Who never had and lost
Forlorn are they
Far more than you and I
Who had and have.
Judge not the price we pay
For love that cannot die.

ALL IS WELL

Death is nothing at all.
I have only slipped away into the next room.
I am I, and you are you.
Whatever we were to each other, we still are.
Call me by my old familiar name,
speak to me in the easy way you always used.
Put no difference in your tone,
wear no forced air of solemnity or sorrow.
Laugh as we always laughed
at the little jokes we enjoyed together.
Pray, smile, think of me, pray for me.
Let my name be ever the household word that it always was.
Let it be spoken without effect,
without the trace of a shadow on it.
Life means all that it ever meant.
It is the same as it ever was; there is an unbroken continuity.
Why should I be out of mind just because I am out of sight?
I am waiting for you, for an interval,
somewhere very near, just round the corner.

HENRY SCOTT HOLLAND
1847-1918

When it seems that our sorrow is too great to be borne,
Let us think of the great family
Of the heavy-hearted into which our grief has given us entrance,
And inevitably,
We will feel about us,
Their arms and their understanding.

HELEN KELLER

YOUR COMPASSIONATE FRIEND

I can tell by that look friend, that you need to talk,
So come, take my hand and let's go for a walk.
See, I'm not like the others, I won't shy away,
Because I want to hear what you have to say.

Your child has died…and you need to be heard,
But they don't want to hear a single word.
They tell you your child's "with God, so be strong."
They say all the "right" things, that somehow seem wrong.

They're just hurting for you and trying to say,
They'd give anything to help take your pain away.
But they're struggling with feelings they can't understand
So forgive them for not offering a helping hand.

I'll walk in your shoes for more than a mile.
I'll wait while you cry…and be glad if you smile.
I won't criticize you or judge you or scorn,
I'll just stay and listen 'til your night turns to morn.

Yes, the journey is hard and unbearably long,
And I know that you think you're not quite that strong.
So just take my hand 'cause I've got time to spare.
And I know how it hurts friend, for I have been there.

You see, I owe a debt you can help me repay.
For not long ago, I was helped the same way.
As I stumbled and fell through a world so unreal—
So believe when I say I know how you feel.

I don't look for praise or financial gain
And I'm sure not the kind who gets joy out of pain.
I'm just a strong shoulder who'll be there 'til the end—
I'll be your Compassionate Friend.

STEVEN L. CHANNING
IN LOVING MEMORY OF:
KIMBERLEY SUSANNE CHANNING
APRIL 15, 1973–FEBRUARY 23, 1987

Our grief always brings a gift.
It's the gift of greater sensitivity and compassion for others.
We learn to rise above our own grief by reaching out
And lessening the grief of others.

REV. ROBERT SCHULER

God knows how much you can bear, and He will not,
if you will only persevere,
allow you to be utterly confounded.

FORBES ROBINSON